ABC WORD BOOK

Children's Picture Book
with
Cool Food and Animals

Written by James Benedict
Illustrated by Abhinav Gupta

ABCDEF
GHIJKL
MNOPQR
STUVW
XYZ

abcdef
ghijklm
nopqrst
uvwxyz

Introductions

ABC Children's Picture Book

Written by James Banadict
Illustrated by Abhinav Gupta

All Rights are Reserved.

ISBN : 978-1-955419-02-4

Emmanuelliteracy.com

Introductions

Have you seen a book with delicious food and unique animals that take you into another world?

This playful ABC Children's Book, an alphabet book, is loaded with happy animals, and a variety of food.

Acknowledgement

I'm thrilled God has helped my son Noah, who endures with brain tumors for many years. Thanks to Abhinav Gupta for the fine illustrations. Also, thanks to Andy Meeks for great proof-reading.

Author

James E. Benedict

Is a teacher, writer, storyteller and the founder of Emmanuel Literacy Foundation. He is the author of kid friendly books including: Unlikely Friends, The Bully's Foe and ABC Word Book. The following books are finished and awaiting publishing: The Contest, The Mystery Box, and A Strange Bed. He is working on many more books. These stories show goodness can come in hopeless situations. James taught in US, Japan and Taiwan for decades at every level from toddlers to University classes.

Contact us   for a Storytelling Seminar.
Email: Emmanuelliteracyfoundation@gmail.com

Ape

Abe the strong ape is hairy.

Avocado

Airplane

An airplane touches the clouds.

Apple pie

Alligator

Bb

Banana cake

Bear

Brown bear is eating a banana.

Books

A pretty bird sings. Bird

Bat

A boat is sailing.

Boat

Cc

Cat

Cheese

The cool cat cooks eggs.

Camel walks in the desert.

Camel

Clock

Our red clock says one.

Chocolate Milk

Cow

"Hot hot!!"

Warm dumplings are yummy.

"I am having a nice ride!"

Dumplings

Duck

The duck can swim or fly.

Ee

Purple Eggplant

Mr. Elk crosses a river.

Peep...Peep.. !!

Elk

Eggs

The gray elephant lifts weight.

Espresso

Elephant

Ff

French Fries

Fish

A fish is sipping lemonade.

Gg

Goose

Goat

Some goats climb rocks and trees.

Hh

Helen the hamster is praying.

Hamster

Hotel

Hippo

Let us have hotdogs and hamburgers!

Hotdog

Hamburger

A horse ran into a hotel.

Horse

Igloo

Iguana family is having a party.

Iguana

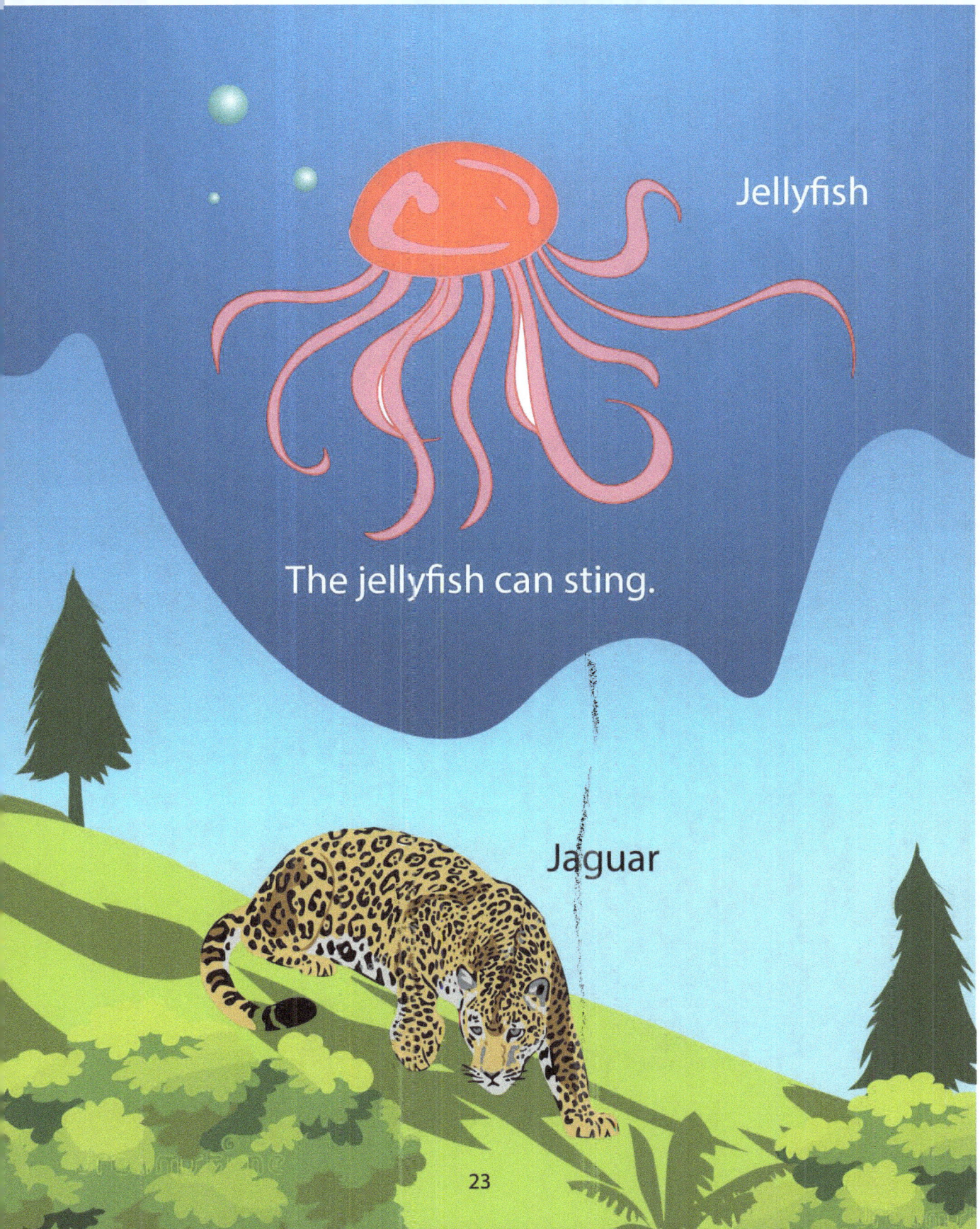

Kk

A kiwi is brown and green.

Koala

Kiwi

Ll

Lollipop

Lion

Strong Lions roar. Grrrrr!

Leek

The yellow Lemon is sour.

Lemon

A happy monster eats a mango.

Nuts

Nighthawk

A nighthawk is flying.

Noodles

Noodles are nice for lunch.

Nightcrawler

Oo

Octopus

An octopus lives in the ocean.

Ostrich

Olivia the owl ate oatmeal for breakfast.

The parrot can say, "Hello."

Hello..!!

Pineapple

Parrot

Quenelle

A quenelle is a french food.

The quail smells a rose.

Quail

Rr

A white rabbit eats rice.

Rice

Rat

Racoon

The racoon has a black mask.

Ramen

Ss

Stawberries

Shark

A shark has many sharp teeth.

Squirrel

In Japan, they eat sushi.

Sushi

Tt

Tea cup

Tacos

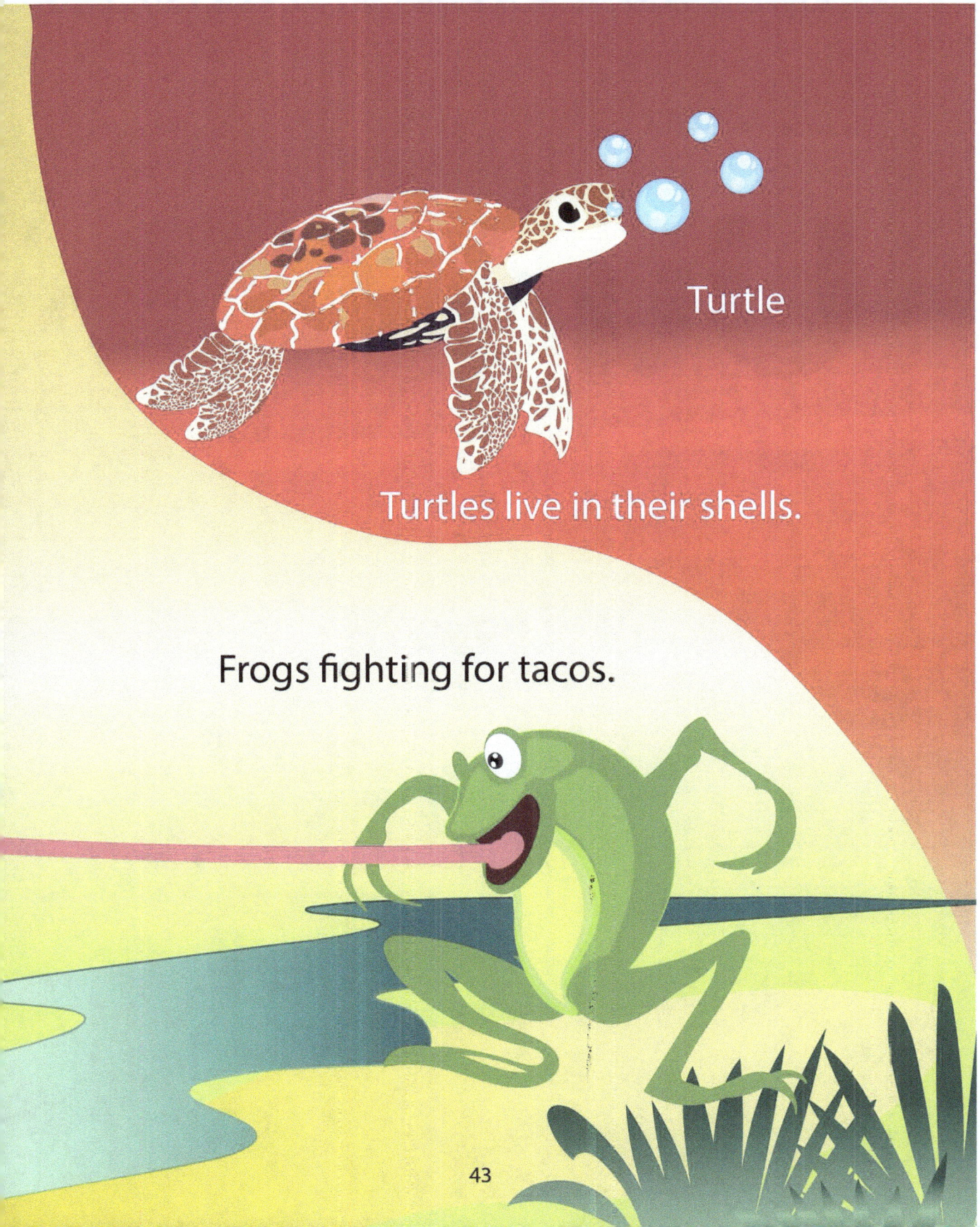

Turtle

Turtles live in their shells.

Frogs fighting for tacos.

Unicorn fish

Our unicorn fish is colorful.

Udon

Udon can be cold or hot.

Vv

Vulture

Mom likes veggie burgers.

Veggie burgers

Vervet

Vipers can be scary.

Viper

Ww

Wasp

Watermelon is good for summer.

Watermelon

(Gigantic)

(Big)

The whale is the biggest animal.

Ax

An ax can open a Durian fruit.

The goat had an X-Ray.

X-Ray

Yam

Yorkie

Yorkie has a beard.

The zebra has stripes.

Zebra

Zuchhini is used for salad.

Zuchhini

An angry zorilla stinks.

Zorilla

Colors

Green avacado

Red apple pie

Yellow Lemons

Voilet eggplant

Orange Fox

Blue Shark

Colors

Black Monster

White egg

Brown bear

Cream velvet

Pink Swan

www.ingramcontent.com/pod-product-compliance
Lightning Source LLC
Chambersburg PA
CBHW082040080526
44578CB00009B/789